A Festive Celebration of

Christmas Joy

Created by
DALE MATHEWS
Arranged by
RICHARD KINGSMORE

BRENTWOOD
MUSIC

Table Of Contents

• •

Companion Product:
Stereo Listening Cassette, **C-5235N**
Stereo Accompaniment Cassette, **TR-3107C**
Split-Track Accompaniment Cassette, **TRS-3107C**
Soprano/Alto Rehearsal Cassette, **C-5235SA**
Tenor/Bass Rehearsal Cassette, **C-5235TB**
Orchestration, **OR-3107**
Conductor's Score, **CS-3107**
Bulletin Covers (100/pack), **BU-3107**
Posters (12/pack), **P-3107**
Cassette/Book Combination, **C/BK-5235**
Christmas Cards/Invitations, **CR-7010**
Christmas Cards with Cassette, **CRC-7010**

Instrumentation:
Flute I and II
Oboe/English Horn (Opt. Clarinet)
Trumpet I, II and III
French Horn I and II (Opt. Alto Saxaphone)
Trombone I
Trombone II (Opt. Bass Clarinet)
Tuba
Percussion I (Mallets, Cymbals)
Percussion II (Tympani, Suspended Cymbals)
Harp
Violin I and II (Opt. Synthesizer String Reduction)
Viola
Cello
Arco Bass
Rhythm (Piano, Bass, Drums, Guitar)

Publication Coordinator/Editor: Penny Bennett

Medley Of Joy

Arranged by Richard Kingsmore

With Excitement

"Sing Joyfully This Christmas Day" (Dale Mathews)

Sing

joy - ful - ly this Christ - mas day, _____ sing

Lyrics:
joy - ful - ly this Christ - mas day, _____ sing

joy - ful - ly this Christ - mas day, _____ sing joy, joy

joy! _____ Sing joy - ful - ly this Christ - mas day,

15 blessed Christmas holiday, glad, glad Christmas is

17 here a-gain. Choirs of angels singing,

19 Christmas bells are ringing, shout the news to all the world that

bells are ringing,

Christ is come!   Sing

joy - ful - ly this Christ-mas day, _____

bless - ed Christ-mas hol - i - day, _____

28
D E/D A/C# Bm A/E E7 A
glad, glad Christ - mas is here a - gain.
30
D D/F# D/A F#m/A D/A G/A
Choirs of an - gels sing - ing,
32
D/A A D/A G D/F#
Christ - mas bells are ring - ing,

shout the news to all the world that Christ is _____

come, _____ shout the news to all the world that

"Joy To The World" (I. Watts, ANTIOCH)

Christ is come.

Sing joy to the world the
He rules the world with

47

D/A　A　D　D/F♯　G　A

Lord is —— come; let earth re - ceive her
truth and—— grace; and makes the na - tions

49

D　G/D　A/D　G/D　D　Em/D　D

King; let ev - 'ry —— heart —— pre -
prove the glo - ries —— of —— His

51

D/F♯　Em7　D　D/A

pare —— Him —— room —— and heav'n and na - ture —— sing, ——
right - eous - ness, —— and won - ders of His —— love, ——

53
D/A G/A D/A G/A Em/A
and heav'n and na - ture sing,
and won - ders of His love,
(2nd time to meas. 63, pg. 12)
55
Em7/A Bm/A Em/A F♯7/A♯ Bm Bm/A G D/F♯ Em7 D G/D
and heav'n and heav'n and
and won - ders, won - ders
58 1.
D/A A7 D D/F♯ G Em7 A(no 3rd)
na - ture sing.
Rit.

12

"Sing Joyfully This Christmas Day"

69 D E/D A/C♯ Bm7 A/E E E7 A

glad, glad, Christ - mas is here a - gain.

71 D D/F♯ D D/F♯

Choirs of an - gels sing - ing, _____

73 G D/F♯ Asus/E Asus/F♯ Asus/G Asus

Christ - mas bells are ring - ing, _____

75 Bm F#m/A G D/F# G D/F# Em7 D Em7 A A#o7

shout the news to all the world that Christ is

77 Bm Bm/A G Bm/F# Em7 D

come. Shout the news to all the world that

79 Em7 A7 D/A Bm/A

Christ is come.

82
Em7/A
A
B♭
B♭/A
Sing
84
Gm7
B♭/F
Em7♭5
Gm/A
N. C.
No Rit.
joy - ful - ly,
sing
No Rit.
87
G/A
A
D
Rit.
(Stop tape)
joy,
joy,
joy!
Rit.

Underscore No. 1

Narrator:

(without music): Welcome to our celebration. A celebration of Christmas Joy! This is a glorious occasion - it's that most wonderful of all seasons, when family and friends, young and old, gather together to rejoice at His coming! *(music begins):* Christmas Joy! You can see it in the face of a child as lights from the tree

sparkle in his eyes. Listen! You can hear it in the sounds of choirs singing and bells ringing out with the joy

of Christmas! It takes us back to a time far removed from here, as we sense the joy of that very first Christ-

mas! Listen! You can hear angels sing joyfully this Christmas day, celebrating the birth of Christ, the new-born King!

Hark! The Herald Angels Sing

Words by
CHARLES WESLEY

Music by
F. MENDELSSOHN
Arranged by Richard Kingsmore

4
C Bb/C C(no 3rd)
mf
F (accented) Gm7 F/A F/C C/Bb
1. Hark! the her - ald an - gels sing,
mf
7
F/A Bb2 F/C C F N. C. F Gm7
"Glo - ry to the new - born King; peace on earth, and
10
F/A G F Dm7/G G G/F C/E G/D C F/C C/G G7 Csus C
mer - cy mild, God and sin - ners rec - on - ciled!"

Joy - ful, all ye na - tions rise, ___ join the tri - umph of the skies; ___ with an - gel - ic host pro - claim, "Christ is ___ born ___ in Beth - le - hem!" Hark! the her - ald

22
Gm D Gm C Am/C Gm/B♭ F/A B♭ F/C C
an - gels sing, "Glo - ry to the new - born
25
F B♭ F/A Gm F C/E D C
mf
F Gm11 C/G
King."
2. Christ, by high - est
mf
28
F/A F/C C C/B♭ F/A B♭ F/C C F
heav'n a - dored; Christ, the ev - er - last - ing Lord!

20

(stagger breathing)

Late in time be-hold Him come,___ off-spring of the
vir-gin's womb: veiled in flesh the God-head see,___
hail th'in-car-nate de-i-ty,___ pleased as man with

40
Gm D Gm C Am/C Gm/B♭ F/A G F F/C C F F/A
men to dwell, Je - sus, our Em - man - u - el.
43
B♭ F/A Gm D Gm C Am/C Gm/B♭ F/A B♭
Hark! the her - ald an - gels sing, "Glo - ry to the
46
F/C C N. C.
new - born King."
Fanfare
f

50

C/D   D

Molto Rit.

Broadly

53 *f* G   Am7   G/B   Cmaj7 D D/C G/B   C2   C

3. Hail the heav'n born Prince of Peace! ___   Hail the Son of ___

Broadly

f (marcato)

56 G/D D G C/D   G   G/F#   Em Em/D A2/C# A/C#

right - eous - ness!   Light and ___ life ___ He brings,

Light and   life   to   all   He brings, ___

Faster
59 Bm A/C♯ D D/F♯ Gmaj7 A Dsus D Am9/D G D/G G
ris'n with heal - ing in His wings. Mild He lays His
Faster
63 Am/G G G/D D G D/G G Am/G G G/D D
glo - ry by, born that man no more may die,
66 C G/B Am E Am D Bm/D Am/C G/B A G
born to raise the sons of earth, born to give them

69 G/D D E E/D C G/B Am E Am
sec - ond birth. Hark! the her - ald an - gels sing,
72 D Bm/D Am/C G/B A G Am7 D9sus D
"Glo - ry to the new - born
75 N. C. C/G D G
ff
(Tape continues)
King!", the new - born King!
Rall.
ff

Underscore No. 2

Narrator:

(music begins): The angel, Gabriel appeared unto the virgin, Mary, who was engaged to Joseph, of the house of David. Sensing she was troubled, the angel said, "Fear not, Mary, for thou hast found favor with God.

And behold, thou shalt conceive and bring forth a son, and shall call His name Jesus. He shall be great and shall be called the Son of the Highest: the Lord God shall give unto Him the throne of His father, David: And He shall reign over the house of Jacob forever; and of His kingdom there shall be no end."

What Child Is This?/Silent Night

Arranged by Richard Kingsmore

"What Child Is This?" (W. C. Dix, Old English Air)

1. What child is this, —— who, laid to rest, on
2. (So) bring Him in - cense, gold and myrrh, come,

Mar - y's lap ___ is sleep - ing? Whom an - gels greet ___ with
peas - ant, king ___ to own ___ Him; the King of Kings ___ sal -

an - thems sweet, while shep - herds watch ___ are keep - ing? ___
va - tion brings, let lov - ing hearts ___ en - throne Him. ___

(Parts both times)

This, this ___ is Christ, the King Whom

shep - herds guard —— and an - gels sing. Haste, haste —— to

bring Him laud, —— the Babe, the Son —— of Mar - y. ——

1.

(to meas. 5, pg. 25) 2.

—— So Mar - y. ——

28

"Silent Night" (J. Mohr, F. Gruber)

Si - lent night,
ho - ly night, Son of God, love's pure light.
Ra - diant beams — from Thy ho-ly face, with the dawn of re-

34
Bm7 Em7 Am7 Am7/D B/D# Em Em/D Em/C#
Rit
deem - ing grace, Je - sus, Lord, at Thy birth,
Rit.
37
a tempo
G/D Dsus D G Em7 G/D
Je - sus, Lord at Thy birth. Je - sus,
a tempo
40
Am Am7/D G/D D G C2/G G (Tape continues)
mp
Rall.
Lord, at Thy birth.
(Off on beat 7 when using track)
mp
Rall.

Underscore No. 3

Narrator:
(music begins): Tonight, we joyously embrace our celebration of Christmas! We rejoice, for this is the birth-

day of the King. We bring to Him our gifts of worship and adoration. Unto Him be all glory and power and

praise as we **tell the story** of His **blessed** birth!

It's The Birthday Of The King

Words and Music by
DALE MATHEWS and ED KEE
Arranged by Richard Kingsmore

We have a story to tell, we have a song to sing, this is mar - ve - lous, glo - ri - ous, won - der- ful news, it's the birth - day of the King! Such

13
B♭ F/A Gm7 F C/E F B♭ F/A Gm7 F
joy - ous news, His bless - ed birth. Re - joice for He brings
16
A7♭9 Dm B♭ C/B♭ F/A Dm7
peace on earth. The an - gels all a - round us sing, it's the
3rd time to CODA
(to meas. 31, pg. 34)
1st time unison ladies
2nd time parts
19
Gm7 C B♭/C F Gm F/A B♭ F/A Gm7 F
birth - day of the King.
1. Re -
2. To

22
mf
C Dm7 C/E
C7
F
B♭
C/B♭
joice, come cel-e-brate His birth, the world has rea-son to
God be glo-ry in the high-est we hear the an-gels
mf
25
F/A Gm7 F
(Parts both times)
B♭
A7
Dm
C/E
sing, for born to-day in Beth-le-hem is
say. Let prais-es ring for Christ, the King is
28
F
G
Csus
C7
D. S. al CODA (to meas. 5, pg. 31)
(repeat 2 times)
Je-sus Christ, the King!
born this Christ-mas day!

CODA
31
F F/E♭ D♭ G♭/B♭ A♭/C D♭
mf
King. Crowned with stars by heav'-nly light,
CODA
mf
34
D♭ G♭/B♭ A♭/C D♭
begin cresc.
F/C C
He left His throne that bless-ed night, won-der of won-ders His
begin cresc.
37
F/C B♭/C Gm11 C
mar-vel-ous love He has giv-en un-to us, He has

40
Am11
D
f
G
Am7
giv - en un - to us.
We have a
f
43
G/B
G
C
D7
G
sto - ry to tell,
we have a song to sing,
this is
46
C
D/C
G/B
D/A
G
A/E
mar - vel - ous, glo - ri - ous,
won - der - ful news, it's the
birth - day of the

Lyrics:

King! _____ Such joy - ous news, His bless - ed birth. Re -

joice for He brings peace on earth. The an - gels all a -

round us sing it's the birth - day of the King. The

58
C D/C G/B G/A G N. C.
an - gels all a - round us sing, it's the
61
Am7 G/B C C/D G
birth - day of the King,
64
Am/D G G E D B A G
(tape continues)
the King!

O Holy Night

Words and Music by
ADOLPHE ADAM
Arranged by Richard Kingsmore

♩ = 66

Unison Choir (optional Solo)

1. O ho-ly night! the stars are bright-ly shin - ing, it is the

night of the dear Sav-ior's birth.

Long lay the world in sin and er - ror

pin - ing, till He ap - peared and the soul felt its

worth. A thrill of hope the

Lyrics: wea - ry world re - joic - es, for yon - der breaks a new and glo - rious morn. Fall on your knees, oh, hear the an - gel

24
Am
Fm/A♭
C/G
G/F
voic - es! O night di -
26
C/E
F
G/F
F
C/E
Dm11
G7
vine, O night when Christ was
28
C
C/G
C/E
G
G/F
C/E
Fmaj7
F6
born! O night, O ho - ly

42

night,   O night di - vine!

2. Tru - ly He taught us to love one an - oth - er; His law is

40
B♭m B♭m/A♭ G♭ E♭m11 G♭/A♭ A♭7 D♭ A♭/D♭
love and His gos - pel is peace.
42
D♭ D♭/F G♭ D♭/F N. C.
Chains shall He break, and in His
Chains shall He break, for the slave is our broth - er,
45
Fm/C C7 Fm
name all op - pres - sion shall cease. Sweet

44

begin cresc.

47 Ebm7/Ab   Ab   Db/Ab   Bbm/Ab   Db/Ab

hymns   of   joy   in   grate - ful cho - rus raise   we,   let

begin building

49 Ebm7/Ab   Ab   Db/Ab   Db/Ab F Eb Db C

all   with - in   us   praise His ho - ly name;

51 f Bbm   Fm

Christ   is   the   Lord,   O

53
E♭m
B♭m
F♯m/A
praise His name for - ev - er! His
55
D♭/A♭
A♭/G♭
D♭/F
G♭
A♭/G♭
G♭
pow'r and glo - ry
57
D♭F
E♭m7
A♭9
D♭
D♭
C B♭ A♭ G F D♭
A♭
A♭/G♭
ev - er more pro-claim! His pow'r and

60
Db/F Gbmaj7 Ebm/Gb Db/Ab Bbm/Ab Ebm/Ab Ab
glo - ry ev - er - more pro -
Faster
62
Db Dbmaj7 Db6 Db Ebm/Db
claim. O ho - ly night,
Faster
65
Ab(no 3rd) Gb/Ab Ab N. C. Cb Cb/Ab Eb Db
ff
Rall.
(Stop tape)
Christ is born!
(Off on beat 6 when using track)
ff Rall.

Angels We Have Heard On High
(Underscore No. 4)

TRADITIONAL FRENCH CAROL
Arranged by Richard Kingsmore

Narrator:

(without music): And there were in the same country shepherds abiding in the field, keeping watch over their flock by night. *(music begins):* And lo, the angel of the Lord appeared to them saying, "Fear not: For behold I

bring you tidings of great joy. And suddenly there was with the angel a multitude of the heavenly host prais-

ing God saying, "Glory to God in the highest, and on earth peace, good will toward men."

48

22
A/E
E
B/E
E
A/E
Why your joy - ous strains pro - long?
26
E
A/E
Say what may the ti - dings be
30
E/B
F#m9/B
B
E
which in - spire your heav'n - ly song?

1st time - unison on melody
2nd time - parts
mf, f
(mel.)
34
E A/B G#m7 C#7 F#m7
Glo - - - - - -
mf, f
38
B E Emaj7 A F#/A# F#m7/B
- - - - - - - ri -
42
B C#m B Amaj7 F#m
1.
E/B
a in ex - cel - sis de -

46
B
B/A
(to meas. 35, pg. 50)
2.
E/B
A/B
B
E
o.
de - o.
50
A/E
B/E
E
53
mf
F
Am7
B♭2
B♭/C
F
See with - in a man - ger laid
mf

57 Dm C B♭maj7 F/A Gm9 Gm9/C C7 F

Je - sus, Lord, of heav'n ———— and earth!

61 Dm Am Gm7 C7 F

Mar - y, Jo - seph, lend ———— your aid,

65 B♭maj7 C/B♭ F/A F Gm7/C C F

with us sing our Sav - ior's birth. ————

1st time - unison on melody
2nd time - parts
69
F
Gm/C
Am/C
Gm/C
C/B♭
f
Am7
(mel.)
Glo -
73
D7
Gm7
C
76
F
Fmaj7
B♭
G/B
Gm7/C
C
ri - a.

(to meas. 72, pg. 53)

80 — Dm — C — B♭maj7 — Gm7 — **1.** F/C — C — C/B♭

in ex - cel - sis de - o.

84 — **2.** F/C — B♭/C — C — *mf* F

de - o.

88 — F — B♭/F — *mf, mp* F

1st time - Men
2nd time - All

Come to Beth - le - hem and see
come, a - dore on bend - ed knee,

mf, mp

Him whose birth the
Christ the Lord, the an - gels sing;

new - born King.

(to meas. 90, pg. 54)

Rit.

(Stop tape)

(Off on beat 5 when using track)

Rit.

Underscore No. 5

Narrator:
(without music): "And this shall be a sign unto you; You shall find a babe wrapped in swaddling clothes, lying in a manger..." This is the message the shepherds heard that night.
(music begins): We're told they rushed to see Him, and having seen Him, they immediately went about telling

everyone all they had seen and heard! Would our response be the same if we heard that Christ were born **to-day?** ... in **our** town? Just down the street - just across town - God's Son - born today! Would we rush to see

Him or would we be too busy with our daily routine to find time for Him? This Christmas season, may we be like the shepherds - always looking for Him, telling everyone we meet what we have seen and heard, bringing

our treasures before Him as we worship Christ the King - for the **Savior** is born **today.**

Away In A Manger/If He Were Born Today

Slightly faster, warmly (♩ = 84)

Arranged by Richard Kingsmore

(Sing 2nd time only) **"Away In A Manger"** (M. Luther, C. Mueller)

58

"If He Were Born Today" (Dale Mathews, Ed Kee)

1. If He were born in a vil - lage to - day,
2. If we could go where the Christ — child lay,

28 Bb   C/Bb   Gm7   C7b9   Dm

if   it   were   not   ver - y   far   a - way,
if   we could hear   what He   longs   to   say,

32 Cm7/F   F/Eb   Cm7/Eb   Bb2/D   Bbm6/Db   (mel.)

would we be - lieve that He was Christ, the King,
would we re - ceive Him as Sav - ior to - day,   or

(mel.)

36 F/C   C/D   Gm7

would   we be too bus - y,   to hear an - gels
would we turn Him a -

(Choir both times)

sing? / way? Would we come and be-

hold the joy He brings, in our

hearts, / in our hearts raise the song / raise the song the an - gels sing? Would we lay our treas-ures be - fore the

King _____ if He were born to - day? _____

(to meas. 24, pg. 58)

day? _____

62

Chords (m. 60): F Bb/F F A G/B A/C# D 4/2 sus Dm

All at once, should ____ we see Him all

Chords (m. 63): C/E C7/E F D/F#

doubt - ing would cease. Noth - ing mat - ters be -

Chords (m. 66): G 4/2 sus Gm G7sus G7 F/G G7 C7sus

side Him, might - y God, Prince of Peace, ____

70
C
D7sus
C/D
D
D6 D7
Molto Rit.
Prince of Peace.
Let us
Molto Rit.
73
a tempo
G
C/G
G2/B
C2
C
come and be - hold the joy He
a tempo
76
Am7/D
Am7
F/A
brings, in our hearts, raise the song the
in our hearts, raise the song
(mel.)

79 an - gels sing. We will lay our treas - ures be -

83 fore the King, ___ the Sav - ior is born to -

87 day. ___ We will lay our ___ treas - ures be -

Rit. *Slower*

91
G/D
D/E
Em7
Am7
Am7/D
D13
fore the King, the Sav - ior is born to -
95
mp
G
Em7
C
Am9
day. The Sav - ior is born
mp
99
Am7/D
G
Gmaj7
Rit.
Am11/G
Am11/D
p
G2
(Stop tape)
to - day!
(Off on beat 6 when using track)
Rit.
p

66

Underscore No. 6

Narrator:
(without music): The prophets had foretold His coming: Behold, a virgin shall be with child, and shall bring forth a Son, and they shall call His name Emmanuel, God with us.
(music begins): The prophet, Isaiah said, "His name shall be called Wonderful Counselor, The Mighty God,

The Everlasting Father, The Prince of Peace... The angel spoke His name to Mary...Jesus, "For He shall

save His people from their sins. Jesus! Name above all names - through Him, those who walked in darkness

His Name Medley
Arranged by Richard Kingsmore

have seen a great light; and through Him, God's Word became life!   "Fairest Lord Jesus" (German Hymn)

Beau - ti - ful

7
A/D D D/C# Bm Bm/A G Em7/A D
Sav - ior! Lord of the na - tions!
10
D2/F# G D/A G D/F# Em7 D2/F# D/F#
Son of God and Son of
13
Em7/A A D2 D G D/A B7 Em
Man! Glo - ry and hon - or,

16 Em/D A/C# G/B Em7/A A D D/F# G2 G

praise, ad - o - ra - tion, now and for - ev - er -

19 D/A A7 G/D D

more be Thine! _____ We'll call Him

"We'll Call Him, Jesus" (Karen Dean)

22 *mf* Em7 Em7/A A7 G/D D A/C#

Je - sus, the name the an - gels whis - pered.

25
Bm7
D/E
Em7
Em7/A
A
G/A
We'll call Him Je - sus, come from heav'n to be our
28
D
C/D
D
G
friend.
We'll call Him Je - sus, the
31
Em7
F♯m/A
G/A
G/D
D
Bm7
sweet - est name in all the world.
We'll call Him

70

Lyrics:
Je - sus, He'll save us from our sin.

We'll call Him Je - sus, the name the an - gels whis - pered. We'll call Him Je - sus, come from

43
heav'n   to   be   our   friend.   We'll call Him

46
Je - sus,_____ the sweet-est name   in   all   the world.

49
We'll call Him   Je - sus,   He'll   save   us   from   our

72

sin.

begin cresc.

Rit.

"At The Name Of Jesus" (C. M. Noel, Jimbo Stevens)

a tempo   1st time - unison on melody
           2nd time - parts

At the name of Je - sus ev - 'ry knee shall

61
Em7 A A7 Dm G Em7 A7
bow, let ev - 'ry tongue con - fess Him
64
Dm Dm7 G C G/F
King of glo - ry now; 'Tis the Fa - ther's
67
Gm7 C F Dm7♭5
pleas - ure that we should call Him Lord,

Who from the be - gin - ning was the might - y

Word. was the might - y Word,

was the might - y Word.

(to meas. 58, pg. 72)

Slight Rit.

Slight Rit.

Come and wor - ship, come and wor - ship,

wor - ship Christ, the new - born

King. Je - sus.

(Tape continues)

(Off on beat 5 when using track)

Rit.

Christmas Festival Medley

Arranged by Richard Kingsmore

With Exuberance

"Good Christian Men, Rejoice" (Tr. J. M. Neale, German Melody)
(Congregation may join 2nd time)

Good Chris-tian men, re-
Chris-tian men, re-

joice———— with heart and soul and voice;———— give ye heed to
joice———— with heart and soul and voice;———— now ye hear of

12 Dm / Dm/C / Bb / F/A / Gm / Am/C / Gm/C

what we say: News! News! Je - sus Christ is
end - less bliss: Joy! Joy! Je - sus Christ was

15 F Gm/C F / F / C/E / Dm / Dm/C

born to - day! Ox and ass be - fore Him bow, and
born for this! He has o - pened heav - en's door, and

2nd time to meas. 25, pg. 78

18 Gm/Bb / Am/C Gm/C F Gm/C F / Bb / C/Bb

He is in the man - ger now: Christ is born to -
man is bless - ed ev - er - more: Christ was born for

78

"God Rest Ye Merry, Gentlemen" (English Carol)

ti - dings of com - fort and joy, com- fort and

joy; O_____ ti - dings of com - fort and

joy._____

"The First Noel" (Traditional)
(Congregation may join)

Lyrics:
first — No - el, the — an - gel did say, was to cer - tain poor shep - herds in fields as they lay; in —

The —

67

D   F#m7   G A/G G D2/F# D Bm/F# F#m7

fields ___ where ___ they lay ___ keep - ing their sheep, on a

71

G A/G G D/F# F#m7 Em   A7   D   A13

cold win - ter's night ___ that was ___ so deep. No -

75 *f*

D   F#m7   D   G ___ *ff* D/A A#o7

el, ___ No - el, No - el, No - el,

born is the King ——— of Is - ra - el.

"O Come, All Ye Faithful" (Latin Hymn, J. Reading)
Majestic

come, all ye faith - ful, joy - ful and —— tri -

88 G/D   D   G/D   Em   D/A   A   D   G/D   D   G

um - phant, O come ye, O come ___ ye to

91 D/A   Asus   A Dsus/A   D   Bm/D   G   Am/G G

Beth - le - hem!   Come   and be-

94 C/E D/F♯   G   D G/D   A/C♯   D   Em/D D   *mf*   N.C.

hold ___ Him,   born the King of an - gels!   O

97 G/D D G/D Am/D G/D D G/D Am/D
come, let us a - dore Him, O come let us a -
mf
100 G/D D/C G/B Am G/B Am/C A7/C♯ D D/C G/B G Cm6/E♭
f
dore Him, O come, let us a - dore Him,
103 Cm6/E♭ G/D Dsus D N. C.
Christ the

(Congregation out)
106 G
A/G G G/D
F/G
G
Lord!
Christ is born to - day!
109 F/G Fmaj7/G G
G/F
E♭
F
Christ is born to - day!
Christ is born, re -
112 ff G
A B♭ A B♭ C C/D G
(Tape continues)
joice!
ff
Rall.

Medley Of Joy
(Reprise)

Arranged by Richard Kingsmore

NOTE: The "Reprise" is an expanded version of "Medley Of Joy". The original may be substituted in its place.

With Excitement

"Sing Joyfully This Christmas Day" (Dale Mathews)

Sing

joy - ful - ly this Christ - mas day, ———— sing

joy - ful - ly this Christ - mas day, _____ sing

joy - ful - ly this Christ-mas day, _____ sing joy, joy

joy! _____ Sing joy - ful - ly this Christ - mas day,

15
G Em7 Em7/A D E/D A/C♯ Bm7
bless - ed Christ - mas hol - i - day, glad, glad Christ - mas is
17
A/E E7 A D D/F♯
here a - gain.
Choirs of an - gels sing - ing,
19
G D/F♯ Bm F♯m/A G D/F♯ G D/F♯ Em7 D
Christ - mas bells are ring - ing, shout the news to all the world that
bells are ring - ing,

Christ is come!

Sing

joy - ful - ly this Christ-mas day, _____

bless - ed Christ-mas hol - i - day, _____

28

| D | E/D | A/C♯ | Bm | A/E | E7 | A |

glad, glad Christ - mas is here a - gain.

30

| D | | D/F♯ | | D/A | F♯m/A | D/A | G/A |

Choirs of an - gels sing - ing, _____

32

| D/A | A | D/A | | G | | D/F♯ |

_____ Christ - mas bells are ring - ing, _____

34
Asus/E Asus/F♯ Asus/G Asus A
36
Bm F♯m/A G D/F♯ G D/F♯ Em7 D Em7 A A♯o7
shout the news to all the world that Christ is
38
Bm Bm/A G Bm/F♯ Em7 D
come,
shout the news to all the world that

"Joy To The World" (I. Watts, ANTIOCH)

Christ is come.

Sing joy to the world the
He rules the world with

47 D/A A D D/F# G A

Lord is —— come; let earth re-ceive her
truth and—— grace; and makes the na - tions

49 D G/D A/D G/D D Em/D D

King; let ev - 'ry —— heart —— pre-
prove the glo - ries —— of —— His

51 D/F# Em7 D D/A

pare —— Him —— room —— and heav'n and na - ture —— sing, ——
right - eous - ness, —— and won - ders of His —— love, ——

53
D/A G/A D/A G/A Em/A
and heav'n and na - ture sing,
and won - ders of His love,
(2nd time to meas. 63, pg. 96)
55
Em7/A Bm/A Em/A F#7/A# Bm Bm/A G D/F# Em7 D G/D
and heav'n and heav'n and
and won - ders, won - ders
58 1.
D/A A7 D D/F# G Em7 A(no 3rd)
na - ture sing.
Rit.

"Sing Joyfully This Christmas Day"

"How Great Our Joy" (Traditional)

69
Bb/F — Fsus — F

joy - ful - ly, joy - ful - ly, sing

71
Eb Eb/D F/C Bb

There shall be born, so He — did say,

73
Gm F Eb Bb/D Bb/C Bb Cm7 F Bb

in Beth - le - hem a (a) child to - day. How

great our joy! Great our joy! Joy, joy, joy,

joy, joy, joy! Praise we the Lord in heav'n on high!

Praise we the Lord in heav'n on high! How heav'n on

"Sing Joyfully This Christmas Day" (Dale Mathews)

More Broadly

Sing joy - ful - ly this Christ - mas day, bless - ed Christ - mas hol - i - day, glad, glad, Christ - mas is

100

Lyrics:

here a - gain. Choirs of an - gels sing - ing,

Christ - mas bells are ring - ing, shout the news to all the world that
bells are ring - ing,

Christ is come. Sing joy - ful - ly this Christ-mas day,

98 | G | Em7 | Em7/A | D | E/D | A/C# | Bm7

bless - ed Christ - mas hol - i - day, glad, glad, Christ - mas is

100 | A/E | E | E7 | A | D | D/F#

here a - gain. Choirs of an - gels sing - ing, ___

102 | D | D/F# | G | D/F#

___ Christ - mas bells are ring - ing, ___

104 Asus/E Asus/F# Asus/G Asus Bm F#m/A G D/F# G D/F# Em7 D

shout the news to all the world that

106 Em7 A A#o7 Bm Bm/A G Bm/F# Em7 D

Christ is ___ come. ___ Shout the news to all the world that

109 Em7 A7 D/A Bm/A

Christ is come.

112
Em7/A
A
B♭
B♭/A
Sing
114
Gm7
B♭/F
Em7♭5
Gm/A
N. C.
No Rit.
joy - ful - ly,
sing
No Rit.
117
G/A
A
D
Rit.
(Stop tape)
joy,
joy,
joy!
Rit.
3

Christmas Joy
Production Notes and Staging Suggestions
by
Jacquelyn Coffey

"Christmas Joy" may be staged effectively in a simple setting with choir and narrator. Or it may be staged more elaborately in a full production using sets, lights, and costumes. The ideas offered here are to encourage your creativity as you consider the resources available in your setting.

Participants:

Singing:
Choir
Mary
Joseph
Shepherd's Choir

Non-Singing:
Narrator
Angel Soloist
Angel Host Movement Choir
Bell Choir (Optional)
A Family: grandparents, mom and dad, teenagers, young children

Costumes:

The Choir, Narrator, Family, and optional bell choir should be dressed in festive contemporary clothing. The rest of the cast should be in Biblical dress appropriate to their character. The Kings could each be robed in different colors, like red, yellow and blue. If you decide to use an entourage of attendants, match their costumes to the color of the King they are attending. This will give you a beautiful procession of color as the Kings and their attendants present the gifts to the baby Jesus.

Setting:

The Choir should be placed in a stationary position in the center back of the stage. The optional Bell Choir could be placed to the Choir's right (stage right) and the Angel Choir could be placed at the Choir's left (stage left). It is best to elevate the Angel Choir on platforms above and behind the Nativity scene. To the far right of the Choir (downstage right) is a warm, homey living room, with a large Christmas tree. The room and the tree will be decorated by the Family during the opening song. To the far left of the choir (downstage left) is the manger. The area directly in front of the Choir (downstage center) is left open. This area will be used for staging the Narrator, Angel Soloist, singing Shepherds, and the three Kings.

(Upstage Center)
Bell Choir   Choir   Angel Choir
(Stage Right)   (Stage Left)
Living room   (Downstage Center)   Nativity
Audience   Audience   Audience

Medley Of Joy

The Choir, Bell Choir and Angel Choir come to their positions on a darkened stage. The lights come up on these performers as the music begins. The Choir sings. The Angel Choir does choreographed arm movements each time the Choir sings: "choirs of angels singing." The Bell Choir plays each time the Choir sings: "Christmas bells are ringing." To be effective in illustrating the words of the song, the Angels and the Bells should only move on their respective phrases. The rest of the time they should hold a posed position until the phrase repeats.

On the musical introduction of **Joy To The World**, the lights build on the living room set, downstage right. Different members of the Family enter carrying Christmas decorations, lights, garland, wrapping paper, and stockings to hang on the fireplace mantle. The Family enthusiastically begins helping each other decorate the room and the tree. This activity needs to be timed out to conclude with the end of the music. The Christmas tree lights are off. They proudly survey their work. On the last bars of the music the "Dad" of the Family lifts the smallest child up to place the Angel on the top of the tree.

Narration

The Narrator moves to downstage center and speaks to the audience. He then looks at the Family enjoying themselves at stage right. On the first note of the musical underscore and with the Narrator's words: "Christmas Joy, you can see it in the face of a child as lights from the tree sparkle..." the Christmas tree lights come on. The children and family members respond enthusiastically. The Narrator then gestures toward the Choir and Bell Choir. The Narrator crosses to downstage left, as he speaks the words: "it takes us back to a time far removed from here." The lights build to reveal Mary and Joseph kneeling beside the manger and the baby Jesus.

Hark! The Herald Angels Sing

On the introduction, the Angels leave their stationary positions on the platforms above the nativity stage left and fill the downstage center area. The lights slowly fade on the living room scene and the manger scene. As the Choir sings, the Angels interpret the words of verses one and three with movement. On verse two the Angels hold a posed position in the direction of the manger. On the last bars of the music the Angels return to their positions above the manger and pose in worship to the King.

Narration

The lights cross fade and go down on the Choir and come up on the Narrator and the Angel Soloist. The Angel is positioned above the manger. As the Narrator speaks, the Angel pantomimes the words spoken to Mary.

What Child Is This?/Silent Night

On the musical introduction the lights cross fade and go out on the Narrator and the Angel. They come up softly on the Choir, and on Mary. She is sitting in the manger area, holding the baby Jesus on her lap.

On the musical seque to **Silent Night**, Joseph enters the manger from stage left. Mary stands and hands the baby Jesus to Joseph. They enjoy Him together. As the song concludes, Joseph places the baby Jesus in the manger. Mary and Joseph kneel beside Him. The manger begins to glow with a soft, warm light, illustrating the words, "radiant beams from Thy holy face." These last movements between Mary and Joseph must be timed to coincide with the last phrase sung by the Choir.

Narration

The lights hold on the Choir and the nativity scene. The lights come up on the Narrator downstage center. He speaks. When he concludes, the lights cross fade and go out on the Narrator, and build to include the Angel Host above the Nativity.

It's The Birthday Of The King

The Choir sings. The Angel Choir is in their stationary positions above the nativity. As the song begins they take a pose with their hands lifted up to heaven. The Angels perform choreographed arm movements each time the Choir sings the phrases: "rejoice," and "the angels all around us sing, it's the birthday of the King..."

O Holy Night

On the musical introduction Joseph slowly stands. The lights cross fade and go out on the Angels, and dim on the Choir. The Bethlehem Star begins to glow above the manger. Joseph looks at the star and begins to sing. During the second verse the singing Shepherds begin to enter the aisles. They are drawn by the Angels and the star. They stop in groups of two and three in the aisles, and look up at the star in front of them.

Narration

The lights come up on the Narrator and the Angel Soloist positioned above the Nativity. As the Narrator speaks, the Angel pantomimes the words, "Fear not..." As the Narrator speaks the words, "and suddenly there appeared a multitude of heavenly hosts...," the lights quickly build to reveal the Angel Choir. The Angel Choir lifts their hands up to heaven in praise of God. The Shepherds in the aisles quickly make their way to centerstage and look up at the Angels in wonder.

Angels We Have Heard On High

The Shepherds turn downstage to face the audience and begin to sing. The lights on the Angels slowly fade.

Narrator

The light comes up on the Narrator stage right. The singing Shepherds move to stage left to look at the baby Jesus. As the Narrator continues to speak, the Shepherds excitedly move out into the aisles to spread the good news. One Shepherd moves from the manger to centerstage. There he meets a Bethlehem couple. They are busy in their everyday chores; sweeping, cooking, etc. The Shepherd pantomimes telling them of the birth of Jesus. He invites them to come and worship. They are too busy and turn back to their chores. He then sees a group of children and invites them to come.

Away In A Manger/If He Were Born Today

The children kneel around the manger. Mary shows them the baby Jesus. The Shepherds begin returning down the aisles. They are carrying baskets of fruit, bread, and other gifts. They stop in the aisles, waiting for their turn to present their gifts to the baby.

On the musical introduction of **If He Were Born Today**, Mary slowly stands and begins to sing. The Shepherds come forward and lay their gifts at the manger. The gifts are presented by small groups. Each group waits until the words, "would we lay our treasures before the King?" are sung. By the end of the song all Shepherds have come to the manger. Some stand and some kneel as they worship the baby Jesus.

Narration

The lights come up on the Narrator. The Shepherds hold their position of worship as the Narrator speaks.

His Name Medley

The lights go out on the Narrator and hold on the Nativity scene as the Choir sings.

Christmas Festival Medley

The Shepherds continue to hold their position of worship. The Choir continues to sing **Good Christian Men, Rejoice**. The three Kings and their entourage process down the aisles as the Choir sings **God Rest Ye Merry, Gentlemen**. They stop in the aisles and wait their turn to present their gifts. As the Choir begins singing **The First Noel,** the Angel Soloist interprets the words with movement. The Angel Choir poses in a position of praise behind the soloist. They remain on the platform above the pose of the Angel Choir in worship to God. They hold this position. As the Choir begins singing **O Come, All Ye Faithful** the Kings move toward the manger. One by one they present their gifts. The Shepherds in awe and wonder move out of the way as they watch the Kings. The Kings kneel in worship and adoration. The Shepherds again move to their position of worship.

Medley Of Joy (Reprise)

As the Choir sings, all in the Nativity scene hold their positions. The Angels repeat their choreography as before. As the Choir begins **Joy To The World,** the lights come up on the living room, stage right. The Family enters the room. They are all carrying various gifts. They give their gifts, and lay them under the Christmas tree. They then embrace one another and turn to face the scene at the manger. They too have come to worship.

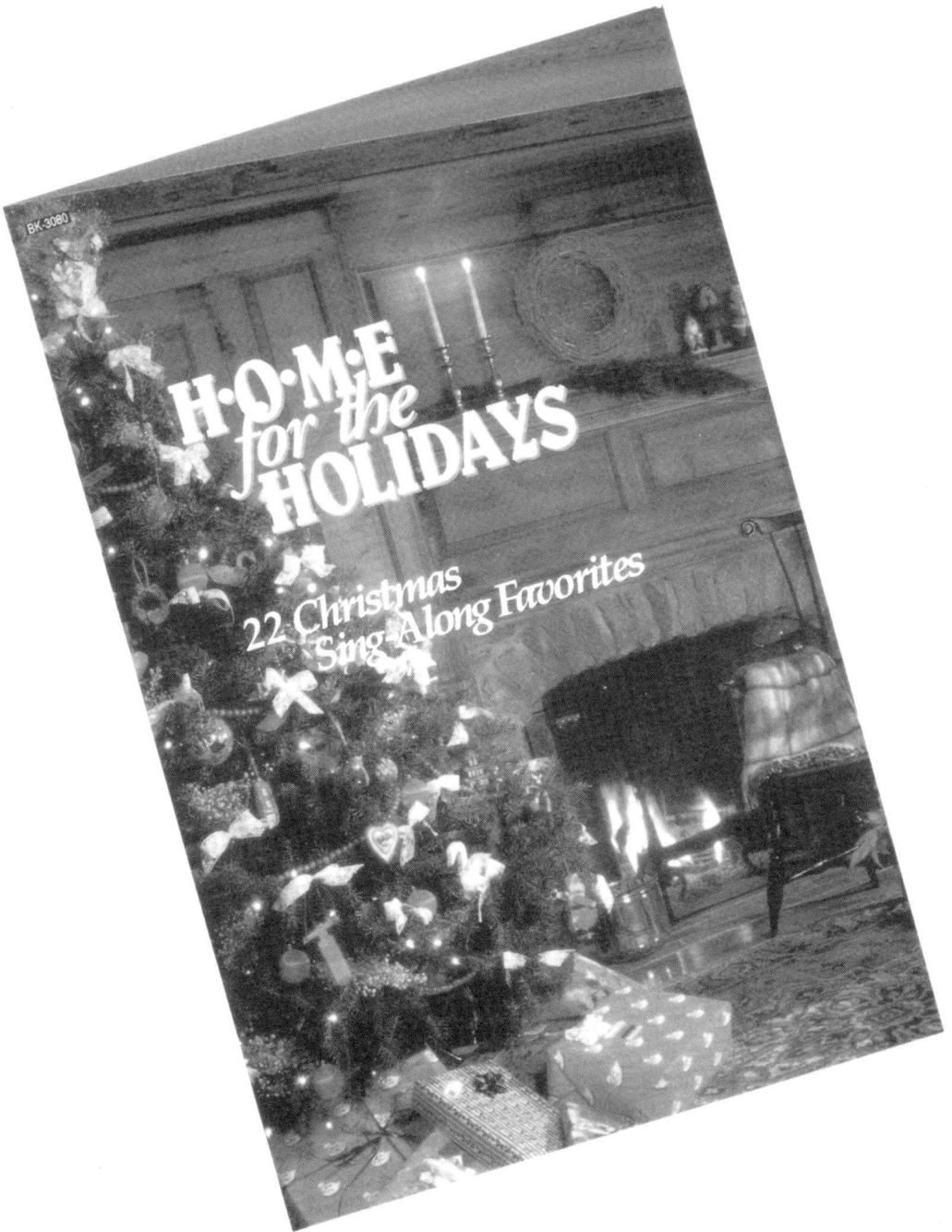

There's no place like home for the holidays, and this exciting recording gives you Christmas like you always remembered it! This wonderful collection of lushly arranged Christmas carol favorites will help you ring in a joyous holiday season! Includes *Joy To The World, Away In A Manger, Angels We Have Heard On High, O Little Town Of Bethlehem, Silent Night* and many more. Arranged by Dave Williamson. Songbook BK-3080.

Companion Product:

Stereo Cassette	C-5195N
Split-track Cassette	C-5161N
Stereo Compact Disc	CD-5195J

Available at Christian music suppliers everywhere.

For more information call

☎ **1-800-333-9000**
Fax 1 (615) 373-0386

BRENTWOOD
═══ MUSIC ═══

316 Southgate Court
Brentwood, TN 37027